MW01165600

"A superb, truly witty and
enjoyable book!"

—The author's Mother

"A pleasurable great read,
vividly written."

—The author's Father

"A disgraceful book, right up there
with trash like *Beavis and Butt-Head,
Roseanne,* and *Married With
Children.* Just how low will our
culture keep sinking?"

—The critics

1

BAD
TASTE
CELEBRITY JOKES

BELLA LA BALLE

Bad Taste Celebrity Jokes

S.P.I. BOOKS
A division of Shapolsky Publishers, Inc.

Copyright © 1994 by Bella La Balle

ISBN 1-56171-232-9

For any additional information, contact:

S.P.I. BOOKS/Shapolsky Publishers, Inc.
136 West 22nd Street
New York, NY 10011
212/633-2022 / FAX 212/633-2123

Manufactured in Canada

10 9 8 7 6 5 4 3 2 1

CONTENTS

CHAPTER ONE
**JOKES ABOUT
HOLLYWOOD
AND CELEBRITIES** 7

CHAPTER TWO
**JOKES ABOUT
GREAT
HISTORICAL FIGURES** 52

CHAPTER THREE
**JOKES ABOUT
FOREIGNERS AND
FOREIGN AFFAIRS** 64

CHAPTER FOUR
**JOKES ABOUT POP
MUSIC STARS** 75

CHAPTER FIVE
**JOKES ABOUT FAMOUS
CRIMES AND CRIMINALS 92**

CHAPTER SIX
**A VARIETY OF
CELEBRITY JOKES 102**

CHAPTER SEVEN
**JOKES ABOUT SPORTS
PERSONALITIES 110**

CHAPTER EIGHT
**JOKES ABOUT
RELIGIOUS FIGURES.............. 130**

CHAPTER NINE
**JOKES ABOUT
POLITICIANS 136**

CHAPTER ONE

JOKES ABOUT HOLLYWOOD AND CELEBRITIES

What did the seven dwarfs say when the prince awoke Snow White from her sleep?

☞ "Guess it's back to jerking off."

☺   ☺   ☺

What does a foot ball and Rosanne Arnold have in common?

☞ Pigskin.

☺   ☺   ☺

Why does Warren Beatty always keep the lights on during sex?

☞ So he doesn't call out he wrong name.

☺   ☺   ☺

Why did Tom and Rosanne Arnold recently consider divorce?

☞ Their doctor put them on a fat-free diet.

☺   ☺   ☺

Why do so many starlets want to date
George Burns?

☞ It's a soft job.

☺   ☺   ☺

What's the difference between Kim
Bassinger and a terrorist?

☞ A terrorist makes fewer
demands.

☺   ☺   ☺

What's the difference between Rosanne
Barr and poultry?

☞ Most poultry is dressed better.

☺   ☺   ☺

What's the only thing that's less exciting than hearing Al Gore speak?

☞ Watching Rosanne Arnold get undressed.

☺   ☺   ☺

Did you hear how Zsa Zsa Gabor got a serious sore throat?

☞ Before letting the doctor paint her throat with medicine, Zsa Zsa insisted on calling her decorator.

☺   ☺   ☺

Exactly how fat is Rosanne Arnold?

☞ On her charm bracelet she
hangs used license plates.

☺   ☺   ☺

Why did Donald Duck ditch Daisy?

☞ He got tired of her quack.

☺   ☺   ☺

Joan Collins was recuperating in a
private suite at the hospital.

Her doctor walked in to check on
her and she asked, "Doctor, darling, I
must know. How long will it be before I
can have sex again?"

"I don't really know," the doctor replied. "NO one's ever asked me that after a tonsillectomy."

☺   ☺   ☺

What did Rock Hudson and Henry VIII have in common?

☞ They both screwed queens—and then died.

☺   ☺   ☺

If Tarzan were Puerto Rican or Arab, what would Cheetah be?

☞ Pregnant.

☺   ☺   ☺

If Tarzan and Jane were Jewish, what would Cheetah be?

☞ A fur coat.

☺   ☺   ☺

What's the difference between vision and sight?

☞ Julia Roberts is a vision;
Rosanne Arnold is a sight.

☺   ☺   ☺

Why did Peter Pan fuck Tinkerbell?

☞ He felt like a fairy tail.

☺   ☺   ☺

Why did Lois Lane suck-off Superman?

☞ Because she knew that happiness was the taste of Kent.

☺   ☺   ☺

Why did Lois Lane divorce Superman?

☞ Turned out he was faster than a speeding bullet in bed, too.

☺   ☺   ☺

Why did Snow White get hired for the soft drink commercial?

☞ Because every night she had seven up.

Why did Liz Taylor fall in love with a construction worker?

☞ A lot more than his hat was hard!

Why was Michael Jackson's chimp

invited to Liz Taylor's wedding?

☞ So the groom would have someone to talk to and hang out with.

☺   ☺   ☺

What's Larry Fortensky's favorite TV show?

☞ *Eight is Enough.*

☺   ☺   ☺

Why has Liz Taylor married eight times?

☞ When she wakes up at night, she's just got to have someone to eat.

☺   ☺   ☺

Did you hear about the new Rosanne Arnold inflatable sex doll?

☞ It's a jumbo plastic garbage can with a pussy in the side.

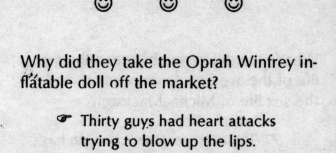

Why did they take the Oprah Winfrey inflatable doll off the market?

☞ Thirty guys had heart attacks trying to blow up the lips.

Why is a tampon like Kim Basinger?

☞ They're both stuck up cunts.

Why is Hollywood madam Heidi Fleiss like Israeli Premier Yitzhak Rabin?

☞ She's a specialist in piece negotiations.

What's the difference between the sex life of the average American man and the sex life of Michael Jackson?

☞ The average American man has had eleven sex partners since the age of 18; Michael Jackson has had eleven sex partners under the age of 18.

Why was Bambi's asshole bleeding?

☞ She'd just made ten bucks.

How did Joan Crawford toilet-train her kids?

☞ She wired 220 volts to their diapers.

☺   ☺   ☺

Who was Tinkerbell's abortionist?

☞ Captain Hook.

☺   ☺   ☺

How did Captain Hook die?

☞ He wiped with the wrong hand.

☺   ☺   ☺

What's worse than Rosanne Arnold with a stomach ache?

☞ Captain Hook with jock itch.

☺   ☺   ☺

What's the proper way to refer to a female private eye?

☞ A Dickless Tracy.

☺   ☺   ☺

Why is Warren Beatty like Joseph of Nazareth?

☞ They both fucked a Madonna.

☺   ☺   ☺

How does Madonna remember how big Warren Beatty's dick was?

☞ She took a dick-tracing.

☺   ☺   ☺

What's Warren Beatty's idea of being unfaithful?

☞ Turning away from the mirror.

☺   ☺   ☺

Did you hear about Disney's planned sequel to the movie Bambi?

☞ It is going to be a stag movie.

Did you hear that Lassie inexplicably went to Denmark?

☞ She came back a cat.

Why is Rosanne Arnold's pussy like Freddy Krueger?

☞ One look at either one will scare the shit out of you.

What kind of bath toy would Madonna buy her kids?

☞ A toaster.

How would Madonna cure her kids of bedwetting?

☞ She'd buy them an electric blanket.

Why didn't Rock Hudson know how he got AIDS?

☞ He didn't have eyes in the back of his head.

Why do aspiring Hollywood gold diggers wear leather pants?

☞ So their crotches will smell like BMWs!

When did Arnold Schwarzeneger realize he was getting a little over-developed?

☞ When he found out he was giving Dolly Parton an inferiority complex.

☺   ☺   ☺

What's "mine shaft?"

☞ What Arnold Schwarzeneger calls his penis.

☺   ☺   ☺

Did you hear President Clinton's latest comments when asked how much he'd spend on defense?

☞ He replied, "It all depends how big de-yard is."

Did you hear about the new airline for senior citizens started by Bob Hope and George Burns?

☞ It's called "Incontinental."

What's the difference between Joan Collins and the Queen Mary?

☞ It takes a few tugs to get the Queen Mary out of her slip.

Did you hear about the movie starring Sylvester Stalone and Rock Hudson?

☞ It's called "Ram-butt."

☺   ☺   ☺

Why did Joan Crawford often take a
clothes hanger to her kids?

    ☞ Because she was angry she
       didn't use it on them before
       they were born.

☺   ☺   ☺

How does Clint Eastwood like his
women?

    ☞ Dirty, and hairy.

☺   ☺   ☺

Who was the little known eighth dwarf
kicked out of the movie for sitting on
Snow White's face?

    ☞ Sleazy.

26

What did Bob Hope sing after Dolly Parton appeared on his show?

☞ "Thanks for the mammaries."

Where do Elvis Presley, John Belushi, Natalie Wood, and Grace Kelly all vacation?

☞ Club Dead.

Why does masturbation make Superman stronger?

☞ He's pumping iron.

How did Ma and Pa Kent know Clark
was wetting the bed?

☞ There was rust on the sheets.

Why will Lois Lane never be anemic?

☞ She gets constant iron
injections.

Did you hear that Robin Leach is endors-
ing a new brand of laxative?

☞ It's for people who want to go
in style.

What do Burt Reynolds and Marilyn Quayle have in common?

☞ They both married dumb blondes.

Did you hear Woody Allen's new girl friend passed away?

☞ It was crib death.

What do you call a Hollywood actress?

☞ Excuse me, Waitress!

☺   ☺   ☺

Did you hear about Woody Allen's new movie which created a controversy because it was titled the same as Michael Jackson's newest album?

☞ They were both called *Close Encounters of the Third Grade.*

☺   ☺   ☺

What's Woody Allen's only objection to having an Oriental lover?

☞ An hour after he fucks her, he's horny again.

☺   ☺   ☺

What does M.A.W. stand for in Hollywood?

☞ Model-Actress-Whatever.

What's the worst-selling celebrity endorsed product of all time?

☞ Arnold Schwarzenegger Toilet Paper—it was rough, tough, and didn't take shit off anyone.

Did you hear Buckwheat became a Moslem when he grew up and changed his name?

☞ He's now "Kareem of Wheat".

What does A.I.D.S. really stand for?

☞ Adios Infected Dick Sucker.

☺   ☺   ☺

What do you call a comedian whose underwear is too tight?

☞ Dickie Smothers.

☺   ☺   ☺

What's Woody Allen and Michael Jackson's 's child-raising philosophy?

☞ "Spare the rod, spoil the child."

☺   ☺   ☺

Did you hear about Zsa Zsa Gabor's new perfume?

☞ It's called "Entrapment"—you slap it on.

What's Pee Wee Herman's favorite restaurant?

☞ The Palm.

What did both Pee Wee Herman and Michael Jackson say when the judge asked them if they wanted a lawyer?

☞ -By coincidence, both replied, "No, thanks—I can get myself off."

What was Kim Bassinger's reply when asked if she smoked after sex?

☞ "I don't know, I never looked."

33

☺   ☺   ☺

Did you hear about the Pee Wee
Herman clothing sale?

☞ The pants are half-off.

☺   ☺   ☺

Did you hear about the new Pee Wee
Herman film?

☞ It's coming in a theater near
you.

☺   ☺   ☺

Did you hear about Pee Wee Herman's
new TV show?

☞ It's called "Different Strokes."

☺   ☺   ☺

Why did E.T. want to get home so badly?

☞ His girl friend's name is E.Z.

☺   ☺   ☺

Did you hear that Oprah Winfrey was arrested for drug possession?

☞ Under her skirt the cops found 50 pounds of crack.

☺   ☺   ☺

How does Oprah Winfrey's fiancé screw her?

☞ He rolls her in flour, then aims for the wet spot.

☺   ☺   ☺

What's the most time-consuming part about humping Oprah Winfrey?

☞ Setting up the on and off ramps.

☺   ☺   ☺

How do we know Cinderella was a virgin?

☞ She always ran away from a ball.

Why did Snow White eat the poisoned apple?

☞ Anything was better than giving those fucking midgets seven blow jobs a night.

☺   ☺   ☺

Why was Batman Returns rated X?

☞ Because we see the Caped Crusader kissing a pussy.

☺   ☺   ☺

What's the difference between the Oscar for "Best Actress" and the Superbowl?

☞ In the Superbowl they kick a punt.

☺   ☺   ☺

What did Woody Allen do when he got really depressed?

☞ He went to one of Mia Farrow's daughters and had her blow his brains out.

☺   ☺   ☺

Warren Beatty was killed in a car crash. A moment later he appeared in the Hereafter, where the Devil was waiting for him. "We're honored to have a celebrity with us," Satan said. "How'd you like a tour?" "Sounds good," the movie star replied. They walked along, and Beatty's eyes grew wide as he saw rooms filled with men sitting at tables covered with fine wine bottles while gorgeous women sat in their laps. He finally turned to the Devil and said, "I had no idea Hell would be like this."

The Devil smiled. "Don't get the wrong idea. See those wine bottles? They all have holes in the bottom." He paused, then continued, "See those women? They don't!"

☺   ☺   ☺

What's Woody Allen's favorite song?

☞ Thank Heaven For Little Girls.

☺   ☺   ☺

What's his (and Michael Jackson's) second favorite song?

☞ Baby Love.

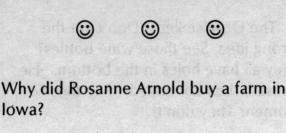

Why did Rosanne Arnold buy a farm in Iowa?

☞ When it's time to eat, she just sprays oil and vinegar on the lawn and grazes.

☺ ☺ ☺

What's six inches long, has a bald head, and drives Heidi Fleiss crazy?

☞ A hundred dollar bill.

☺ ☺ ☺

What's 12 inches and white?

☞ Nothing..

Why didn't Burt Reynolds ever take Loni Anderson out to dinner?

☞ Burt made it a rule never to date married women.

Why did Burt Reynolds learn to lie with a straight face?

☞ So he could lie with a curved body.

Did you read that Loni Anderson bought a new set of towels?

☞ They read "Hers" and "Hers Soon."

41

Warren Beatty was sitting poolside at the Beverly Hills Hotel downing double Scotch after double Scotch when a friend came up and said, "Warren, what's wrong? You look terrible."

Beatty sighed and said, "It's what happened this morning. I came out of my agent's office when this young girl came up to me and asked for a handout. It was pouring rain, but she was shivering in this ragged tank top and a short skirt. She told me that all her money had been stolen, she'd been evicted from her apartment, and she hadn't eaten for days."

"That sounds depressing," the friend said.

"Yeah," Beatty answered. "I could barely hold back the tears while I was fucking her."

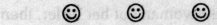

Burt Reynolds and the girl he picked up were undressing in a hotel room when the woman said, "You know, all the guys I've been with have had pet names for their cock—Dick, John, Harry, etc. What do you call your cock?"

Reynolds, replied "My cock doesn't need a name."

"Why not?"

"Because," he replied, "even without a name, mine always comes when it's called."

☺   ☺   ☺

Winona Ryder, Michelle Pfeiffer, and Rosanne Arnold walked into a lingerie shop to buy new set, of panties. The saleswoman asked the teenage Ryder how many she needed.

"Seven," the young thing replied, "One for each day of the week."

43

The saleswoman got her order, then asked the same question of Pfeiffer.

"I need one each day for Monday through Friday," the sex symbol said. "On weekends, my lover and I spend so much time in bed I don't need panties."

The saleswoman gave her five pair, then said to Rosanne, "How many pairs do you need?"

"12," she replied. "January, February, March...."

☺   ☺   ☺

Why did Tom Arnold trade his wife for an outhouse?

☞ The hole was smaller and it smelled so much better.

☺   ☺   ☺

What do investment bankers and Heidi Fleiss have in common?

☞ They both promote mergers.

☺   ☺   ☺

Loni Anderson was sitting in her lawyer's office and the attorney said, "I don't think it helped your case that you hit Burt over the head with a lamp."

Loni said, "He humiliated me. He barged into my bedroom and called me a nymphomaniac."

"Is that a reason to hit him?"

"It sure was," she replied. "He said it in front of the gardener, the pool boy, and my personal trainer."

45

Why is Cindy Crawford like a mail order sex aid?

☞ They're both effective penis enlargers.

Why doesn't Rosanne Arnold wear yellow?

☞ So people don't shout "Taxi" at her.

How many Hollywood starlets does it take to screw in a light bulb?

☞ Go fuck yourself, dude.

Why did National Geographic Magazine publish nude pictures of Oprah Winfrey?

☞ So gorillas could masturbate, too.

Why did Bugs Bunny's girl friend refuse to screw him?

☞ She was having a bad hare day.

Why are Heidi Fleiss's call girls like defense contractors?

☞ They both charge $1,000 for a screw.

Where did Heidi Fleiss write her memoirs?

☞ In a loose-life notebook.

Why is Madonna like the Panama Canal?

☞ They're both very busy ditches.

What happens if you're on a yacht with Madonna and a storm comes up?

☞ You get blown ashore.

☺　　　☺　　　☺

What sign did Heidi Fleiss put over the door of her new Beverly Hills house?

☞ "Grand Opening Sale."

☺　　　☺　　　☺

Did you hear about the financial problems at the Sesame Street t.v. show?

☞ Things got so bad they had to make fast money shooting a kiddie porn movie called, Sesame Street Presents: *Swallow That Bird*.

☺   ☺   ☺

Why didn't Cinderella wear panties?

☞ So the Prince could see if it fit.

☺   ☺   ☺

What's blue and red and spins around and around?

☞ A smurf in a blender

☺   ☺   ☺

Did you hear about the death that was caused by a bunch of rich, spoiled high school students?

☞ Someone was hit by a car and they dialed 9-0-2-1-0 by mistake.

Did you hear about the new Mel Brooks movie starring Michael Jackson, Eddie Murphy and Richard Pryor?

☞ It's called *Blazing Sambos*.

What do you get when you cross Joan Collins and a pit bull?

☞ The last blow Job you'll ever get.

What is Miss Piggy's special douche filled with?

☞ Hogwash.

CHAPTER TWO

JOKES ABOUT GREAT HISTORICAL FIGURES

What did Henry VII say to his lawyer?

☞ "Screw the divorce. I've got a better idea for the bitch."

☺   ☺   ☺

Did you hear about the great artist with brown fingers?

☞ His name was Pic-ass-o.

☺   ☺   ☺

What did Satan really say to Eve when he handed her the apple?

☞ "Eat this—it'll make your tits bigger."

☺   ☺   ☺

What kind of illumination did Noah use on the Ark?

☞ Flood lights.

☺   ☺   ☺

Why did Adam and Eve often argue?

☞ She was always putting his pants in the salad.

☺   ☺   ☺

How do we know Abe Lincoln was Jewish?

☞ He was shot in the temple.

☺   ☺   ☺

Why was Oedipus's mother mad at him?

☞ Because he was hard on her.

☺   ☺   ☺

After following Jesus around for months, Marry Magdalene finally got him in the sack. It turned out the Son of God was a fabulous lover, and the former prostitute was in ecstasy as she came time after time. Finally, Jesus shot his load, rolled off, and fell into a deep sleep.

Mary was anxious for more. She lay beside him for hours, massaging him all over and cooing in his ear. Finally, she reached under his robe and detected signs that he was stirring. She was so excited that she got up, ran into the room where the Apostles were sleeping, and shouted the famous words, "Christ has risen, Christ will cum again!"

☺   ☺   ☺

Who was the world's first bookkeeper?

☞ Adam. He turned over a leaf and made an entry.

☺   ☺   ☺

What was God's second mistake?

☞ A woman.

Why wasn't John F. Kennedy such a good boxer?

☞ He couldn't take a shot to the head.

How do we know Oedipus's mother was so open-minded?

☞ She did everything under the son.

What did God do on the 8th day of Creation?

☞ He began answering complaints.

What was unique about Presidents George Washington and Thomas Jefferson?

☞ They were the last two white men to have those surnames.

What was the one consolation for Jackie the day after John F. Kennedy was assassinated?

☞ Some of his brains finally rubbed off on her.

☺   ☺   ☺

Who really assassinated JFK?

☞ 500 Iraqi sharpshooters with machine guns.

☺   ☺   ☺

How did Stevie Wonder pierce his ears?

☞ Answering the stapler.

☺   ☺   ☺

What's the first question Helen Keller asked her teacher when she learned to communicate?

☞ "Are your tits bigger than mine?"

What did the sadist do after he raped Helen Keller?

☞ Cut off her hands so she couldn't yell for help.

Why does Stevie Wonder have one black leg and one yellow?

☞ His dog is blind, too.

Why didn't Helen Keller make noise when she fell down the stairs?

☞ She was wearing gloves.

☺   ☺   ☺

What was Helen Keller's major speech impediment?

☞ Calluses.

☺   ☺   ☺

How did Helen Keller's teacher penalize her for talking in class?

☞ Made her wear mittens.

☺   ☺   ☺

Why doesn't Stevie Wonder ever change his baby's diaper?

☞ So he can find him easily.

Why does Helen Keller masturbate with one hand?

☞ So she can moan with the other.

Why didn't Stevie Wonder's bicycle have a front wheel?

☞ So he could feel the road.

What's the cruelest present Stevie Wonder got?

☞ Rubik's cube.

☺ ☺ ☺

What's the second cruelest present Stevie got?

☞ A paint-by-number set.

☺ ☺ ☺

What's the cruelest present Stevie ever gave?

☞ His first paint-by-number picture.

☺ ☺ ☺

What did Helen Keller consider oral sex?

☞ A manicure.

☺ ☺ ☺

How did Helen Keller burn her hands?

☞ Answering the oven.

☺ ☺ ☺

What's black and crispy and comes on a stick?

☞ Joan of Arc.

☺ ☺ ☺

Why couldn't Mozart find his teacher?

☞ He was Haydn.

CHAPTER THREE

JOKES ABOUT FOREIGNERS AND FOREIGN AFFAIRS

What do the airlines do with used vomit bags?

☞ Donate them to Bosnia Relief and take a tax write off.

☺   ☺   ☺

What goes "hop, skip, jump, boom?"

☞ Bosnian children playing in a mine field.

How do Iraqi and Hezbollah soldiers keep their bayonets sharp?

☞ By always keeping a dead baby on the tip.

☺ ☺ ☺

How do they take the census in Bosnia?

☞ They add up the number of arms and legs and divide by 2.

Saddam Hussein was sitting at his desk, an aide came in and told him U.S. cruise missiles had knocked out his security headquarters as well as a few houses in a residential zone.

The Iraqi leader rose to his feet, face red with anger. "Those infidels!" he swore. "Slaughtering innocent men, women, and children. Who does Clinton think he is—me?"

☺   ☺   ☺

Did you hear that Boy George had sex with a member of the Royal Family?

☞ Rumor has it he had Prince Albert in his can.

☺   ☺   ☺

How can you tell Prince Charles is horny?

☞ He's got a stiff upper lip.

The British Royal Family was on safari in Kenya and had camped for a night in the bush. One of the guides was assigned to keep guard. Some time after midnight, the guide heard a thrashing near the Royal Tent. He rushed off, and a few minutes later several shots were heard.

When the guide returned to the campfire, Prince Philip was waiting for him. "Tell me, my good man," the prince inquired, "what was that commotion about?"

"I heard a noise," the guide replied. "When I went to investigate, I saw the outline of this horrible figure with broad shoulders, an equine face, and an enormous rear end. So I aimed and fired several times."

"My God, man!" the Prince exclaimed. "You've shot the Queen!"

Did you hear that Imelda Marcos committed suicide?

☞ She piled up all her shoes, then jumped.

What kind of punishment did the government have in mind for Imelda Marcos?

☞ Living in a cell for ten years with Manuel Noriega.

What's the difference between the World Trade Center bombers and a box of shit?

☞ The box..

How can you make a Bosnian refugee feel at home?

☞ Bomb his bedroom.

Why is Saddam Hussein's Iraq such a unique place?

☞ It's the only country where a man can really talk his head off.

☺   ☺   ☺

Is it unfair that people say Princess Anne looks like a horse?

☞ Not really when you consider her gynecologist is a vet.

Why is Queen Elizabeth so popular in India?

☞ Hindus worship the cow.

Did you hear that Queen Elizabeth grew up thinking sex was evil?

☞ When Prince Charles was born, she had her proof.

Why did the new Iraqi Navy purchase 20 glass-bottom boats?

☞ So they could see the old Iraqi Navy.

☺   ☺   ☺

Why is Saddam Hussein like Little Miss Muffet?

☞ They both had Kurds in the way.

☺   ☺   ☺

Did Adolf Hitler wipe his ass with his left hand or his right hand?

☞ With toilet paper—he wasn't that crazy.

☺   ☺   ☺

What were Princess Grace's last words?

☞ "You fool, I said `Bud Lite,' not 'Hard right!'"

☺   ☺   ☺

What's the latest fashion in Bosnia?

☞ Tank tops.

☺   ☺   ☺

What's the worst part about massacring
a thousand Chinese students?

☞ An hour later, you feel like massacring a thousand more.

☺   ☺   ☺

What's was the biggest obstacle in nego-
tiating the North American Free Trade
Agreement with Mexico?

☞ Finding a wall large enough for
them to write it on.

☺   ☺   ☺

Princess Diana was in labor all night. Finally, Prince Charles rushed to Buckingham Palace, was admitted to the Queen's chamber, and announced, "Your majesty, there is a new member of the royal family."

The Queen said, "Congratulations, Charles. Is it a boy or a girl?"

The Prince said, "I really don't know—they haven't dressed it yet."

☺   ☺   ☺

What do you get when you cross John Gotti with the President of Mexico?

☞ A guy who makes you an offer you can't understand.

☺   ☺   ☺

Why did Princess Diana called Prince Charles a "hobosexual?"

☞ He was a bum fuck.

☺   ☺   ☺

Why will L.A. riot victim Reginald Denney not receive justice for his near murder?

☞ Because the fate of his attackers is in the hands of 12 people too stupid to get out of Jury Duty.

CHAPTER FOUR

JOKES ABOUT POP MUSIC STARS

How does Madonna keep her youth?

☞ She locks him in the closet during the day.

Why hasn't Dolly Parton ever been the Playboy centerfold?

☞ Because you'd never be able to close the magazine.

☺   ☺   ☺

What's the difference between Madonna's hair and her male lover?

☞ Both are blown dry every day.

☺   ☺   ☺

Why is Madonna like a Tootsie Pop?

☞ They're both terrific suckers.

☺   ☺   ☺

What is Madonna?

☞ Living proof that women are never satisfied.

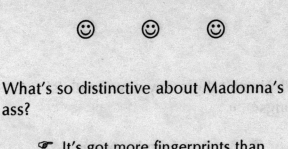

What's so distinctive about Madonna's ass?

☞ It's got more fingerprints than the F.B.I.

What looks like a male rock star, acts like a male rock star, and talks like a male rock star?

☞ A female rock star.

What's so unique about Madonna's anatomy?

☞ She has no private parts.

☺   ☺   ☺

Why aren't there any new Beatle's songs?

☞ Because John Lennon is de-composing.

☺   ☺   ☺

What's endless love?

☞ Stevie Wonder playing tennis with Ray Charles.

☺   ☺   ☺

What's the difference between a proctologist and a Hollywood actress?

☞ A proctologist only has to deal with one asshole at a time.

Why was Madonna voted entertainer of the year by the American Medical Association?

☞ Because her movies make people so sick.

Why does Madonna have insomnia?

☞ She just can't keep her thighs closed.

Why hasn't Madonna visited Mount Rushmore?

☞ She can't decide which face to sit on.

Did you hear that Madonna did a pilot for a TV sitcom?

☞ It's called "I Love Loosely."

Why doesn't Dolly Parton make topless movies?

☞ They'd flop.

Why is Dolly Parton the luckiest woman in the world?

☞ Her cup runneth over.

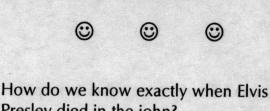

How do we know exactly when Elvis Presley died in the john?

☞ He left a log.

What did the talent scout say about Dolly Parton?

☞ "She's got a great future ahead of her."

If Elvis Presley were on stage today, how would he do?

☞ He'd stink.

81

Why can't Boy George tell dirty jokes?

☞ When he's alone, he's in mixed company.

Did you hear about the Whitney Houston scandal?

☞ They found nude pictures of her parents in National Geographic.

What game does Michael Jackson like to play with his young friends?

☞ Show and smell.

Why does Michael Jackson spend so much time with young boys?

☞ He wants to give them a head start.

Why does Michael Jackson disappear for an hour after one of his young friends leaves?

☞ It takes him that long to get the bubble gum off his cock.

What's the difference between Bill Clinton, Dan Quayle and Jane Fonda?

☞ Jane went to Viet Nam.

What do Somalians and Yoko Ono have in common?

☞ They both live off dead beatles.

What do you call Barbara Streisand's pubic hair?

☞ Yentl floss.

What makes Michael Jackson nostalgic?

☞ Thinking about blowing his first nose.

Why did Michael Jackson want to look like a woman?

☞ His dick was only 10 inches long.

What's the difference between Mr. Potato Head and Michael Jackson?

☞ Michael Jackson has had more noses.

What do Michael Jackson and paper napkins have in common?

☞ They've both been dyed white.

☺   ☺   ☺

What's the difference between a limousine and Madonna?

☞ Not everyone's been in a limousine.

☺   ☺   ☺

What looks like a dog and has wings?

☞ Linda McCartney.

☺   ☺   ☺

Why is fucking Madonna like investigating a plane crash?

☞ In both cases, you're probing for the black box.

Where is the best place for Dolly Parton to hide something from her husband?

☞ In her forehead.

Did you hear about the world's dumbest mosquito?

☞ He bit Dolly Parton on the arm.

What do you call a bisexual bathroom?

☞ Elton John.

Did you hear that Liberace and Rudolph Nureyev both really died of food poisoning?

☞ They ate too many bad wienies.

What do you get when you cross a cat with Mick Jagger?

☞ A pussy with big lips.

Did you hear that Michael Jackson's lover passed away?

☞ It was crib death.

Why is Madonna immune to men?

☞ She's been inoculated so many times.

Why did Dolly Parton stop entering beauty pageants?

☞ She was tired of getting the booby prize.

Why does Madonna wear NASA panties?

☞ She thinks her ass is out of this world.

☺   ☺   ☺

Did you hear that Dolly Parton decided to burn her bra?

☞ It took the fire department four days to put out the braze.

☺   ☺   ☺

The doctor finished examining Michael Jackson. He called the superstar into his office and said, "Michael, you know that I can't reveal our private conversations because of doctor-patient confidentiality. So I want you to tell me why you're fooling around with little boys again."

Jackson said, "I couldn't help myself—but how did you know?"

"Why else would you have a GI Joe figure shoved all the way up your ass?"

How can you tell you're at a Madonna concert?

☞ The usher flashes you on the way in.

CHAPTER FIVE

JOKES ABOUT FAMOUS CRIMES AND CRIMINALS

What do you call a severed head, two arms, and a liver?

☞ Jeffrey Dahmer's ex-boyfriend.

Did you hear about the guy who took early retirement from the Three Mile Island nuclear power plant?

☞ He went to Maine and got a job as a lighthouse.

How did Washington, D.C. honor ex-Mayor Marion Barry?

☞ They gave him the kilos to the city.

How did the F.B.I. become suspicious of former Washington mayor Marion Barry?

☞ He tried to snort the White House.

How does the dictionary define "white trash"?

☞ With a picture of Beavis and Butt-Head.

93

What did Jeffrey Dahmer and cemetery workers have in common?

☞ They both dig dead people's holes.

How do you get into the Jeffrey Dahmer fan club?

☞ You have to show your dismember-ship card.

What is the biggest crime committed by Boy George?

☞ Male Fraud.

☺   ☺   ☺

Why was Ted Bundy's mother so disappointed in him?

☞ He never dated the same girl twice.

☺   ☺   ☺

Why was Ted Bundy like a bad golfer?

☞ He always took a few slices before he put it in the hole.

☺   ☺   ☺

What's the worst thing you could say to Jeffrey Dahmer?

☞ "Over my dead body."

95

What does Dr. William Kennedy Smith tell all his female patients?

☞ "Take two margaritas—and call me."

What's the only idea that is as frightening as Dan Quayle becoming president?

☞ William Kennedy Smith becoming a gynecologist.

Did you hear that Rodney King was arrested in Los Angeles?

☞ The charge was "impersonating a pinata."

☺   ☺   ☺

What's the difference between Rodney King and Pee Wee Herman?

☞ Pee Wee Herman beats himself.

☺   ☺   ☺

Why did William Kennedy Smith decide to become a gynecologist?

☞ He wanted to look up his old girlfriends.

☺   ☺   ☺

The wealthy industrialist suffered a heart attack and was confined to bed for several weeks. One day his doctor came to see him and said, "I've got some good news and some bad news."

The rich patient said, "Give me the good news first."

The doctor said, "I was wrong about your prognosis. You've bounced back amazingly well. As I told your wife a few minutes ago, while you'll have to stay in bed or use a wheelchair, I think you've got some quality time ahead of you."

"That's terrific," the man exclaimed. "What could possible be the bad news?"

The doctor said, "Your wife just fired me. Your new doctor's name is Kevorkian."

☺   ☺   ☺

What's so unusual about having drinks at the World Trade Center?

☞ You stay sober, but your car gets bombed.

Why did the Los Angeles police officers leave the ball game early?

☞ They wanted to beat the crowd.

How does Ted Bundy's family honor his memory?

☞ Every year they lay a wreath on the fuse box.

Jeffrey Dahmer walked into a psychiatrist's office and said, "Doc, whatever I tell you is confidential, right?"
The shrink said, "Absolutely."
Dahmer said, "Then I have to tell you

99

that these incredible urges come over me sometimes. I go out, pick up a black faggot, bring him back to my apartment, torture him for hours, kill him, fuck his dead body, then cut up the corpse and keep the parts in the refrigerator. The next day, I feel tremendously guilty."

"That's the most shocking thing I've ever heard. Of course, I'll help you to control those urges."

"That's not why I'm here," the serial killer replied. "I want to work on getting rid of these terrible feelings of guilt."

What did they say when they strapped Ted Bundy into the electric chair?

☞ "More power to you."

Why was Jeffrey Dahmer like a taxidermist?

☞ Whenever he found anything dead, he mounted it.

Does the Pope shit in the woods?

Is the bear Catholic?

Does Jeffrey Dahmer go to the fridge when he wants a piece of ass?

CHAPTER SIX:

A VARIETY OF CELEBRITY JOKES

Why is the Hubble Space Telescope like ten martinis?

☞ They both make the night sky fuzzy.

☺   ☺   ☺

What do you call it when Gloria Steinem goes to the bathroom?

☞ A feminist movement.

What do you call it when Ralph Nader goes to the bathroom?

☞ A consumer movement.

What do you call it when the Pope goes to the bathroom?

☞ A religious movement.

What is the ideal "hot date" in Hollywood?

☞ A blonde nymphomaniac who does you and then turns into a pizza and a 6-pack at midnight!

What happened after Wall Street hotshits like Mike Milliken went to jail?

☞ So far, ten prisons have merged, three have gone private, and two others bought airlines.

How do you know when Santa's a pervert?

☞ When he unzips his fly and says, "Wanna be Santa's little helper?"

Did you hear about the new Teamster doll?

☞ Wind it up and it steals your pension fund.

Did you hear about the new Teamster doll?

☞ Wind it up and it steals your pension fund.

What's Ivana Trump's favorite sex aid?

☞ A bank book.

How did Claus von Bulow get rich?

☞ It was just a lucky stroke.

☺   ☺   ☺

Why is Ralph Nader so humorless?

☞ He can't recall jokes.

☺   ☺   ☺

What happened after a group of savings and loan executives were sentenced to jail?

☞ Six months later, two million license plates were missing.

☺   ☺   ☺

What car does Elvis drive most often?

☞ The Legend.

What do Fred Flintstone and the residents of South Central Los Angeles have in common?

☞ They both live next door to rubble.

Why shouldn't we be surprised when shrinks have sex with their patients?

☞ What other kind of person would use the term "The-rap-ist."

What's brown and sits in the woods?

☞ Winnie's Pooh.

What was Humpty Dumpty's last thought?

☞ "Oh, my goodness, I'm not wearing clean underwear."

☺　　☺　　☺

Did you hear that General Motors is re-naming its pick-up trucks with side-gas tanks?

☞ They're now known as "chariots of fire."

☺　　☺　　☺

What's "egghead?"

☞ What Mrs. Dumpty gives to Humpty.

Why didn't they cremate Colonel Sanders?

☞ They couldn't decide whether to do him regular or extra crispy.

What's worse than having magician David Copperfield pull a rabbit out of your hat?

☞ Having him pull a hare from your snatch.

CHAPTER SEVEN

JOKES ABOUT SPORTS PERSONALITIES

How did Mike Tyson meet Robin Givens?

☞ One day he opened his wallet, and she was there.

☺   ☺   ☺

How did Tom Watson's wife straighten out his putter?

☞ She licked his balls.

Why was Robin Givens always black and blue?

☞ Mike Tyson always knocked before he entered.

Why were Robin Givens and Mike Tyson considered a fastidious society couple?

☞ She's fast and he's hideous.

What baseball team did Bill Clinton and Dan Quayle both play for?

☞ The Dodgers.

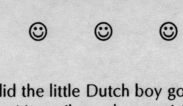

Why did the little Dutch boy go see Martina Navratilova play tennis?

☞ He wanted to stick his finger in a dyke.

What do John Gotti and Pete Rose have in common?

☞ Four thousand hits.

What's a George Steinbrenner sandwich?

☞ One that's so full of baloney you can't swallow it.

☺   ☺   ☺

Why is Bill Clinton like a diaper?

☞ He's always on somebody's ass, and he's usually full of shit.

☺   ☺   ☺

What's a "Fuck-off?"

☞ The selection process for the Dallas Cowboy Cheerleaders.

☺   ☺   ☺

What would you get if you slipped amphetamines to Bobby Knight?

☞ A prick that stayed up all night.

Did you hear that President Clinton just created 12,000 new jobs for blacks?

☞ He added 1,000 teams to the N.B.A.

What's eternity?

☞ The length of time until a white man wins the N.B.A. slam dunk competition.

Why did the Boston Celtics think Len Bias was a wildflower?

☞ Two days after they picked him, he died.

How do you make the Len Bias All-Star Basketball team?

☞ You have to be six-feet-and-under.

Where's Len Bias playing basketball now?

☞ We don't know, but there must be stiff competition.

Why does Martina Navratilova have the cleanest cunt in tennis?

☞ She had her maid come three times a day.

How do we know that Martina Navratilova is popular on the women's tennis circuit?

☞ Because all women eat her up and no man is down on her.

What has fuzzy balls and eats pussy?

☞ Martina Navratilova.

What does Martina Navratilova do when her opponent makes a mistake?

☞ Gives her a tongue lashing.

☺   ☺   ☺

Does Martina Navratilova like to cook?

☞ She prefers eating out.

☺   ☺   ☺

Why does Martina Navratilova call her girlfriend "Creme de Menthe?"

☞ She's her favorite licker.

☺   ☺   ☺

What nourishment sustains Martina Navratilova during a tennis tournament?

☞ Box lunches.

How does Martina Navratilova pick up another female tennis player?

☞ She compliments her on a nice set.

When did the other tennis players suspect Martina Navratilova was gay?

☞ When she came into the locker room and said she'd lick every woman in the place.

What car do people with tax problems, like Willie Nelson's, drive?

☞ The Dodge

What did actress Jodi Foster say to her girlfriend?

☞ "Your face or mine?"

Why does Martina Navratilova love soybeans?

☞ She's into meat substitutes.

What do Mohammed Ali's brain, Mike Tyson's brain and a zucchini have in common?

☞ They're all different types of squash.

119

☺   ☺   ☺

What's the definition of "gibberish?"

☞ A conversation between Joe
   Louis and Mohammed Ali.

☺   ☺   ☺

Did you hear about the new Mike Tyson
perfume for women?

☞ You slap it on.

☺   ☺   ☺

What do you call a speech by
Mohammud Ali?

☞ Racial slurs.

Why does Martina Navratilova spend so much time in Europe?

☞ She misses her native tongue.

If homosexuals got AIDS from butt-fucking, how did the Los Angeles Laker girls get AIDS?

☞ By magic.

Did you hear about the new Magic Johnson porno flick?

☞ It's called, *Lethal Weapon 4.*

When did Magic Johnson's wife suspect he'd contracted a sexually transmitted disease?

☞ When he began to dribble before he shot.

Did you hear about Evil Knievel's lastest stunt?

☞ He's going to run across Somalia with a large sandwich strapped to his back.

What's Billy Martin doing now?

☞ Managing the Angels.

How did they bury Billy Martin's casket?

☞ Umpires kicked dirt over it.

What does seven foot tall Kareem Abdul Jabbar and Michael Jordan do now that they're retired?

☞ Go to movies and sit in front of you.

Why did Mike Tyson plead temporary insanity at his rape trial?

☞ When he got a hard on, there was no blood left to go to his brain.

☺   ☺   ☺

Why did the New York Rangers change their name to the New York Tampons?

☞ They're only good for one period and they have no second string.

Why did the football coach sign up Madonna and Sister Teresa?

☞ He needed a wide receiver and a tight end.

Denver Broncos' quarterback John Elway looked upon himself as a Greek god, and he resented having to undergo the physical exam required at the beginning of the season. When it was his turn to see the team doctor, he swaggered in and said arrogantly, "Doc, this is a waste of time. If you find anything wrong with me, I'll get you four seasons tickets on the 50 yard line."

"Fair enough," the doctor replied. He spent nearly half an hour, poking and proding and listening with his stethoscope. Finally, he even made the quarterback bend over and stuck two fingers up his ass. But he still didn't find anything wrong.

"Give up, doc?" Elway smirked.

"One more test. Open your mouth."

When the quarterback complied, the doctor inserted the two fingers he'd used for the rectal exam. Elway gagged and vomited noisily on the floor.

"Ah!" the doctor exclaimed. "Weak stomach."

☺   ☺   ☺

Why did Eddie Murphy and Wilt Chamberlain have sex on their minds all the time?

☞   Because their heads are covered with pubic hair.

Why did Robin Givens divorce Mike Tyson?

☞ Mr. Right turned out to be Mr. Right Hook.

What did the lesbian say when Martina Navratilova and Helena Sukuva wanted to screw her at the same time?

☞ She demanded separate Czechs.

What's Martina Navratilova's life like on the pro tennis tour?

☞ She muffs a few strokes on the court, then strokes a few muffs in the locker room.

☺ ☺ ☺

What's the difference between Elvis and Salmon Rushdie?

☞ Elvis lives.

☺ ☺ ☺

What's stranger than Moby's dick?

☞ Lucille's balls.

What do you call K.D. Lang, Martina Navratilova, and Lily Tomlin?

☞ A menage a twat.

Did you hear that General Motors is re-naming its pick-up trucks?

☞ They're now known as "chariots of fire."

Why don't Iraqi schools mix drivers' education with sex education?

☞ It would wear the shit out of the poor camels!

CHAPTER EIGHT

JOKES ABOUT RELIGIOUS FIGURES

What's the only good thing to come out of the Branch Davidian fire in Waco?

☞ David Koresh finally stopped smoking.

☺   ☺   ☺

Did you hear that the Branch Davidians changed their name?

☞ They're now the Ignited Church of Christ.

Did you hear about the new Branch
Davidian charcoal?

☞ Your fire will be simply divine.

Why was being a Branch Davidian such
a lousy job?

☞ No matter what a person did,
he ended up being fired.

☺   ☺   ☺

What does Jerry Falwell eat when he's
constipated?

☞ Moral fiber.

Why did all the necrophiliacs, along with Jeffrey Dahmer, rush to Waco?

☞ They heard about some really hot pieces of ass.

Did you hear about Tammy Faye Bakker's new make-up kit?

☞ It comes with three gallon cans and an ice-cream scoop.

Did you hear what Minnie Mouse bought Mickey for his birthday?

☞ A Bill Clinton watch.

What happened when Tammy Faye Bakker scraped off her make-up?

☞ They discovered that underneath she was Jimmy Hoffa.

What is Jimmy Swaggart's new commandment?

☞ "Thy shalt not use thy rod on thine staff."

☺   ☺   ☺

What does the M.A.G.I.C. in Magic Johnson's name really stand for?

☞ My Ass Got Infected Coach.

Why are we better off because Jimmy Swaggart and Jim Bakker were TV evanglists?

☞ Until them, we didn't really know what sin was.

Did you hear about new sex magazine created by evangelist Jimmy Swaggart?

☞ It's called "Re-Penthouse."

What was Jim Bakker's favorite Christmas carol?

☞ "Cum, All Ye Faithful."

What was Jimmy Swaggart's favorite religious activity?

☞ The laying on of hands.

Why was Jimmy Swaggart like a hog farmer?

☞ They both paid $50 for a pig.

Why can we be sure Adam and Eve were happily married?

☞ Adam didn't have to listen to his wife complaining about the guy she could have married.

135

CHAPTER NINE

JOKES ABOUT POLITICIANS

☺   ☺   ☺

Did you hear that Bill Clinton has created a new cabinet post devoted to women's affairs?

☞ It's called the Secretary of the Inferior.

Why is President Clinton just like a busy fag?

☞ In both cases, the source of their popularity is going down.

☺ ☺ ☺

How can you tell if a guy likes to spend all his time alone?

☞ If he joins the Dan Quayle, Jim Bakker, or Jimmy Swaggart Fan Club.

☺ ☺ ☺

President Clinton wasn't feeling well, so he called the White House Doctor for an exam. The physician poked and prodded for a few minutes. Clinton finally asked, "Doc, can you tell me what's wrong?"

The doctor said, "Well, as far as I can tell, you've got a chronic fecal impaction."

"What does that mean?" the President asked.

"You're perpetually full of crap."

Tired of his low approval ratings, President Clinton called up the head of the CIA and said, "I want your very best agent over here first thing in the morning." Moments later, a call went out to the Middle East, and the most talented American agent was recalled back to Washington.

The next morning, the agent was escorted into the Oval Office. The President said, "I hear you're the best in the business. I can't trust what my staff tells me, so I want you to visit every state and every single major city. I want you to stay out on the road until you have an idea of what the vast majority of Americans would like to see happen in the Oval Office. Understand?"

The CIA agent responded affirmatively. He left the White House and wasn't heard, from for nearly four months. Finally, he showed up early on Saturday morning, and the President saw him immediately. President Clinton said, "Did you find out what an overwhelming majority of Americans want done here in this office?"

"Yes, sir."

"Well, then, express the will of the people," Clinton ordered.

So the agent then stood up, pulled out a gun, and shot the President.

Why is the post office raising the price of stamps again?

☞ They need the money to buy more "This Window is Closed" signs.

What would happen if you merged Domino's Pizza with the U.S. Postal Service?

☞ Your pizzas would arrive four days late.

☺   ☺   ☺

Why is Congress so tough on criminals?

☞ When it comes to stealing, they don't like competition.

☺   ☺   ☺

If the band plays "Hail to the Chief" when the President enters a room, what do they play when a Congressmen comes in?

☞ "Send in the Clowns."

☺   ☺   ☺

Why can't you circumcise an Iraqi?

☞ Cause there is no end to those pricks.

What was the difference between Election Day and Thanksgiving Day?

☞ On Thanksgiving, we get a turkey for the day; on Election Day, we get a turkey for four years.

The struggling actor was turned down for part after part, and he'd nearly given up. Then one day an agent called and said, "I got the word that they're casting a play about President Kennedy. I remembered that you resemble him quite a bit."

The actor said, "People have told me that. I'd do anything for a part right now."

The agent said, "With your lack of

credits, there's only one way you can succeed. I want you to throw yourself into the role. Read every book ever written about Kennedy. Go through all the newspapers from his presidency. Watch every video tape of him you can find. Then talk like him, dress like him, act like him every minute."

The actor followed that advice, slaving away 24 hours a day until he almost believed he was John F. Kennedy. Finally, the day of the audition came, and the actor was so caught up in the arrogance of being Kennedy that he was brilliant. To his great joy, he got the big part.

And on the way home, he was assassinated.

☺   ☺   ☺

The guy at the bar turned to his buddy and said, "You know, I really miss Ronald Reagan."

His friend said, "How can you say

that? All the presidents are alike—they say and do absolutely nothing."

"Yeah," the first guy retorted. "But when Reagan said nothing, you knew he really meant it."

☺   ☺   ☺

How thin is Nancy Reagan?

☞ They sent her picture to Somalia, and the Somalians sent back food.

☺   ☺   ☺

How do we know George Bush abuses his wife?

☞ He stays married to her.

Why did Dan Quayle do so badly in school?

☞ The only letter he bothered learning was "I."

Why does Dan Quayle enjoy having a cold?

☞ It's the only thing he can keep in his head for more than five minutes.

Why is the Clinton Administration like cocktail party refreshments?

☞ They're both an assortment of nuts.

How cold was it last winter?

☞ So cold that Bill Clinton actually slept with Hillary to keep warm.

Why is Dan Quayle like an interstate highway?

☞ They both have a big yellow stripe down the middle.

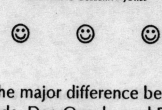

What's the major difference between Jane Fonda, Dan Quayle, and Bill Clinton?

☞ Jane Fonda spent more time in Vietnam.

Why did George Bush really select Dan Quayle as his running mate?

☞ Because when you go fishing for voters, you need a worm.

Why is Dan Quayle like a skeleton?

☞ Neither one has any guts.

Why is President Reagan like a high-class Washington call girl?

☞ He's slept with nearly every important Republican—except he did it during Cabinet Meetings.

What's this? (Hold up a blank piece of paper.)

Did you hear about Ross Perot's plan to solve our biggest urban problem?

☞ It's called, "AIDS for the Homeless."

Why does Ronald Reagan call Nancy "Mummy" in bed?

☞ She's dry as dust and hasn't moved in 2,000 years.

☺   ☺   ☺

How senile is Former President Reagan getting?

☞ Last week, he forgot the Alamo.

☺   ☺   ☺

Did you hear about the new Jessie Jackson bumper sticker?

☞ It says "RUN, JESSIE, RUN—IN '96", and you put it on the front of your car.

What's the difference between a Republican woman and a Democratic woman?

☞ A Republican woman has Bush in her heart and a Democratic woman has Hart in her bush.

What does Ronald Reagan mean when he complains about not getting enough action?

☞ His prune juice isn't working.

Did you hear that when Jesse Jackson became successful, he decided to help his family by hiring his mother to clean his house?

☞ Unfortunately, he had to fire her because she stole things from him.

What was the worst mistake Gary Hart made with Donna Rice?

☞ Not letting Ted Kennedy drive her home.

151

What's the definition of "redundant?"

☞ Telling Ronald Reagan to "forget it."

What did Clarence Thomas find the hardest part about being a Supreme Court Judge?

☞ Fitting a watermelon in his briefcase each day.

Why did Clarence Thomas always have sex on the brain?

☞ Because his head is covered with pubic hair.

His clerk was surprised one day when Supreme Court Justice Clarence Thomas walked in wearing a tuxedo. "What's up, Judge?" he asked.

Justice Thomas said, "I have an appointment to get a vasectomy."

"So why the tuxedo?"

"Because if I'm gonna be impotent, Goddamit, I want to look impotent."

What's Justice Clarence Thomas's idea of foreplay?

☞ "Yo, wake up, bitch."

What's Andrew Dice Clay's idea of fore-play?

☞ Snapping his fingers while say-ing, "On your knees, bitch!"

☺ ☺ ☺

What's so remarkable about Justice Clarence Thomas?

☞ He's a black man who has a job and can name his children.

Why did George Bush nominate Clarence Thomas to the Supreme Court?

☞ So the F.B.I. could finally find out if he'd been fucking Barbara.

How did Justice Sandra Day O'Connor welcome Clarence Thomas to the Supreme Court?

☞ She let him inspect her briefs, then insisted he put his staff to work.

☺   ☺   ☺

What major contribution did Justice Clarence Thomas make to the Supreme Court?

☞ Every Friday, he brings in his *Long Dong Silver* porno videos for the office to watch.

☺   ☺   ☺

Did you hear about the new Hillary Clinton inflatable sex doll?

☞ You have to fill it with ice water.

How do you recognize the new Nancy Reagan inflatable sex doll?

☞ It has no pussy.

What's the only way to warm up Nancy Reagan?

☞ Cremation.

What's the proper term for the Reverend Jesse Jackson and the Reverend Al Sharpton?

☞ Holy Shit.

Where do you find Ted Kennedy after a dozen Scotches?

☞ On the floor of the Senate.

Why did they carry a live monkey on Dan Quayle's plane?

☞ In case the Vice-President needed spare parts.

Why was Dolly Parton so jealous of the Republican party?

☞ Bush and Quayle beat her in the "biggest boobs" contest.

Why were Ronald Reagan and George Bush "ethnosexuals?"

☞ They loved to fuck over blacks and Puerto Ricans.

What's the difference between Hillary Clinton and Joan Collins?

☞ Hillary Clinton specializes in snow jobs.

What does news anchorman Dan Rather have in common with panty-hose worn inside-out?

☞ They both rub Bush the wrong way!

Why does Bill Clinton regularly treat the American people like mushrooms?

☞ Because he likes to feed us a lot of shit and then keeps us in the dark.

What's Dan Quayle's idea of helping the handicapped?

☞ Issuing "I am not a camel" signs to the hunchbacks of America.

What's the best way to render Dan Quayle speechless?

☞ Ask him what he thinks.

Why is Dan Quayle like the Jolly Green Giant?

☞ They're both prominent American vegetables.

161

How can you tell if you're in Janet Reno's bedroom?

☞ Her vibrator is a cattle prod.

What are Jesse Jackson's chances of being elected President?

☞ Outstanding—if the Republicans nominate Saddam Hussein.

How did Bill Clinton finally manage to slow down inflation?

☞ He turned it over to the Post Office.

Why is Dan Quayle so much in demand as a speaker guaranteed to raise money at Republican fund raisers?

☞ The organizers charge $100 a head to get in—and $200 to get the Fuck out of there..

Why did Dan Quayle refuse when George Bush asked him to go on a round-the-world trip?

☞ He said he'd have no way of getting back.

☺   ☺   ☺

Why was Ronald Reagan the most efficient U.S. President?

☞ Every day he got in eight hours of work and eight hours of sleep—and he still had sixteen hours left over.

☺   ☺   ☺

Did you hear Dan Quayle finished his first book?

☞ Reading it, not writing it.

What do Ross Perot's grandchildren do at Christmas?

☞ Sit on Santa's lap and ask him what he needs.

What did Dan Quayle do when President Bush ordered him to tour Central America?

☞ He immediately made reservations to go to Illinois, Iowa, and Kansas.

Why did Dan Quayle sign up for Latin classes?

☞ President Bush ordered him to Latin America.

Why wasn't anyone surprised Ronald Reagan got nose cancer?

☞ He always had his head up his ass.

Did you hear about the new toilet paper with President Clinton's picture on every sheet?

☞ That's so the assholes can see exactly who they voted for.

What's the caption on a picture of Presidents Jimmy Carter, Jerry Ford, and Richard Nixon?

☞ "See no evil, hear no evil, and evil."

What happened when Nancy Reagan heard about the famine in Somalia?

☞ She was so upset she had to go out and spend $10,000 on new clothes.

Why did George Bush cancel his plans to add his face to Mount Rushmore?

☞ The Army Corps of Engineers told him there wasn't room for two more faces.

Did you hear that Bill Clinton finally found a job for Jesse Jackson?

☞ He's going to be U.S. Ambassador to the Bermuda Triangle.

When was the only time in history that the White House telephone was disconnected?

☞ During the Bush Presidency. When the phone bill came in, Bush vetoed it.

What's the main difference between the Dan Quayle of ten years ago and the Dan Quayle of today?

☞ Ten years ago, Quayle was a little-known incompetent politician; today, he's a well-known incompetent politician.

What do re-electing Ted Kennedy and saving the whales have in common?

☞ They both help preserve wild life.

How does one sleep like a typical politician?

☞ First you lie on one side, then you lie on the other....

What's black and brown and would look great on Beavis and Butt-Head?

☞ Two Dobermans.

What's the difference between one useless man, two useless men, and three or more useless men?

☞ One useless man is a disgrace; two useless men are a law firm; three or more useless men are called The Clinton Administration.

Election day business was slow at the whorehouse, so the madam sent one of her girls outside to attract some attention. Whenever a car passed, she'd lift up her skirt and caress her pussy. A lot of drivers pulled over, parked, and went inside.

Then an unmarked police car went by. A moment later, a detective was clamping handcuffs on the hooker. The madam rushed out and said, "You have no right to do that."

The cop replied, "Of course I do. She was engaging in lewd behavior. That's illegal."

The madam said, "She was doing no such thing. She was expressing a political opinion, and free speech is absolutely legal."

"Free speech? She put her finger in her pussy, then put it up to her nose."

"That's right," the madam said. "She was saying, 'President Bush stinks!'"

What's the difference between the Iraqi Army and Senator Ted Kennedy?

☞ Ted Kennedy has at least one confirmed kill.

Did you hear that Hollywood is making a movie on the subject of rape when Senator Kennedy and William Kennedy Smith are in Palm Beach?

☞ It will be called *Bill and Ted's Excellent Adventure Part Two.*

What's Bill Clinton's political philosophy?

☞ "If they're too young to vote, fuck 'em!"

Did you hear about the new film about Dan Quayle's military career?

☞ It's called *Thirty Seconds Over Indianapolis*?

What do you get when you cross a Kennedy and a Jew?

☞ An alcoholic who buys his liquor wholesale.

What do you get when Sandra Day O'Connor gives you a blow job?

☞ An honorable discharge.

What do an Irishman and John F. Kennedy, Jr. have in common?

☞ They both had a great deal of difficulty passing the bar.

☺ ☺ ☺

Why is a postal worker just like a rifle with a broken firing pin?

☞ It won't work and you can't fire it.

☺ ☺ ☺

What does the U.S. Post Office and Thom McCan's shoe-stores have in common?

☞ 500,000 black loafers.

Why was the 1992 Democratic Presidential ticket "R-rated?"

☞ Too much sex and Gore.

Why are the Clinton's like a fag couple?

☞ There are two pricks in the bedroom.

Why was Bill Clinton so anxious to move his family to Washington?

☞ In Arkansas, Chelsea would be married and pregnant at 13.

177

What do Ross Perot the and a Yugo car have in common?

☞ They're both small and ugly, and you never know when they're going to quit on you.

Why is the Clinton Administration like a wet dream?

☞ They're both coming unscrewed.

One Friday night around midnight, Bill Clinton wandered over to the Executive Offices and discovered his young staffers were throwing a wild party. He saw that a white sheet with a hole in it had been strung across one of the offices. A secretary explained, "The guys took turns sticking their dicks through the hole, and we had to guess their identity."

The President said, "Sounds like fun. Wish I'd been here."

"You should have been," the girl replied. "Your name came up eight times."

What do Bill Clinton and baseball pitchers have in common?

☞ Fast balls.

Why will the big influx of women in Congress help end the recession?

☞ We won't have to pay them as much.

How many Kennedy's does it take to rape a girl?

☞ Two. One to rape her and one to swear it never happened.

Why do the Clintons always fuck doggie style?

☞ So they can both watch CNN during sex.

Why does it take Ted Kennedy half an hour to change a light bulb?

☞ He holds the bulb in one hand, then drinks until the room spins.

Why did John F. Kennedy, Jr. flunk his bar exam twice?

☞ He kept thinking an anti-trust suit was a chastity belt.

What's the difference between Rush Limbaugh and a hypodermic needle?

☞ None. They're both a pain in the ass.

181

☺   ☺   ☺

Why did everyone accuse Ronald Reagan of indifference toward minorities?

☞ He though Taco Bell was the Mexican phone company.

☺   ☺   ☺

What has four legs and two breasts?

☞ The American presidency.

☺   ☺   ☺

What's the difference between Liberace and Bill Clinton?

☞ Clinton's aides haven't killed him yet.

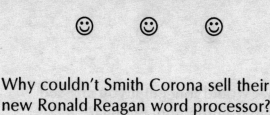

Why couldn't Smith Corona sell their new Ronald Reagan word processor?

    ☞ It had no memory and no colon.

What would you call the kids if Connie Chung married Jesse Jackson?

    ☞ "Chiggers."

Why does Dan Quayle display his college transcript on his dashboard?

    ☞ So he can park in the handicapped space.

What would you get if you crossed Hillary Clinton and a gorilla?

☞ Nothing—there are some things even a gorilla won't do.

What's the best way to describe Attorney General Janet Reno?

☞ She looks like she ran out of money halfway through a sex change operation.

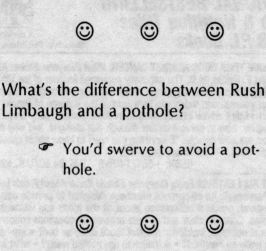

What's the difference between Rush Limbaugh and a pothole?

☞ You'd swerve to avoid a pothole.

What's the difference between Hillary Clinton and JAWS?

☞ Nail polish.

What's so special about the White House elevator?

☞ It's the only thing that Hillary Clinton will go down on.

ADDITIONAL BESTSELLING
Health & Nutrition Titles
from S.P.I. Books

A division of
Shapolsky Publishers, Inc.

☐ **IMPROVE YOUR ODDS AGAINST CANCER: *What Everyone Should Know*** by **John F. Potter, M.D.** The nationally acclaimed founder of the Vincent Lombardi Cancer Research Center details valuable information on how to protect yourself and those you love against the scourge of cancer. Dr. Potter's explicit advice includes how to evaluate doctors, early prevention techniques, how to prevent cancer through diet changes, and why most cancers are now curable. "Everything you need to know about cancer in a single book." — *The Washington Post*
(ISBN: 1-56171-076-8 – U.S. $4.50/U.K. £2.99)

☐ **WHAT AM I EATING? *Facts Everyone Should Know About Foods*** by **Dr. Mia Parsonnet.** An all-purpose handbook designed to provide easy-to-understand, practical information about all the foods and vitamins we consume. Contains clear and concise answers to questions concerning food and nutrition, including: are fast foods really so bad? • are health foods really so healthful? • is it wise to use bottled water? • what is the record of vitamin supplements? Dr. Parsonnet has compiled an essential handbook for anyone concerned about their diet.
(ISBN: 1-56171-034-2 – U.S. $12.95/U.K. £7.50)

☐ **STOP THE NONSENSE: *Health Without the Fads*** by **Dr. Ezra Sohar.** For everyone confused by the newest fads and "latest" discoveries about what's good for us and what's not, this books cuts through the clutter and delivers the straight facts. Dr. Sohar calls upon us to develop a logical, "life-style approach" to good health based on solid scientific evidence, reducing the confusion from the latest, often contradictory, medical advice. "...offers a common sense approach to health and nutrition... contrasts favorably with all the recently promulgated fads on dieting."—Jean Mayer, President, Tufts University, Chairman (fmr.), White House Conference on Nutrition & Health
(ISBN: 1-56171-006-7 – U.S. $16.95/U.K. £9.99)

Buy them at your local bookstore or use this convenient coupon for ordering.
S.P.I. BOOKS • 136 West 22nd Street • New York, NY 10011
Telephone: 212-633-2022 • FAX 212-633-2123

Please send me the books I have checked above. I am enclosing $ _____
(please add $1.95 to this order to cover postage and handling—50¢ for each additional book). Send check or money order—no cash or C.O.D.s. Make checks payable to S.P.I. Books. New York State residents please add appropriate sales tax.

Name _____

Address _____

City _____ State _____ Zip Code _____
Allow 2 to 3 weeks for delivery.

Recent S.P.I.
Entertainment Books

SWEETHEARTS: 156171-206-X $5.50 U.S./ $6.50 CANADA
☐ The inspiring, heartwarming and surprising stories of he girls America tuned in to watch every week in the '60's these glamorous and sexy stars who made the '60's a time to remember and long for:

Goldie Hawn & Judy Carne- "Laugh-In's" funniest girls
Mary Tyler Moore- "The Dick Van Dyke Show's" Laura Petrie
Sally Field- "Gidget's" Frannie Lawrence & "The Flying Nun's" Sister Bertrille
Elizabeth Montgomery- "Bewitched's" Samantha Stevens
Barbara Eden- "I Dream of Jeannie"
Tina Louise & Dawn Wells- "Gilligans Island's"
Diana Rigg- "The Avengers'" Emma Peel
Stefanie Powers- "The Girl from U.N.C.L.E."

COSBY: 156171-205-1 $4.99 U.S/$5.99 CANADA
☐ The Critically Acclaimed Revealing Look at America's #1 Entertainment Legend Cosby. Packed with revealing interviews with friends, family and other stars plus sixteen pages of exclusive photos.

Chronicles Cosby's early struggle up from Philadelphia's projects and his tireless efforts to break through the color barriers in show business and build an unmatched career.

Cosby's illustrious list of triumphs in the last 25 years are revealed as well, including his marriage and family and a Grammy and Emmy award-winning TV, recording and film career, including YOU BET YOUR LIFE.

To order in North America, please sent this coupon to: **S.P.I. Books** •136 W 22nd St. • New York, NY 10011 • Tel: 212/633-2022 • Fax: 212/633-2123

Please send European orders with £ payment to:
Bookpoint Ltd. • 39 Milton Park • Abingdon Oxon OX14 4TD • England • Tel: (0235) 8335001 • Fax: (0235) 861038

Please send____books. I have enclosed check or money order for $/£ (please add $1.95 U.S./£ for first book for postage/handling & 50¢/50p. for each additional book). Make dollar checks drawn on U.S. branches payable to S.P.I. Books; Sterling checks to **Bookpoint Ltd.** Allow 2 to 3 weeks for delivery.
☐MC ☐ Visa # _____
Exp. date _____
Name _____
Address _____

SPI EXPOSÉS
The Truth Behind the Story

The Kennedy Brothers
Behind the Scenes
From SPI Books